Marxism in Plain and Simple English
The Theory of Marxism in a Way Anyone Can Understand

BookCaps™ Study Guides

www.bookcaps.com

Table of Contents

Introduction

In Chapter 7 of his infamous book, *Das Kapital* (or Capital), Karl Marx quotes the old proverb, "The road to hell is paved with good intentions." Little did he realize when he wrote those words that his own well-intended creations, socialism and Marxism, and their offshoot, communism, would end up creating a hell on earth for millions of working people in the Soviet Union, China, and the eastern side of the Berlin Wall. Even today, Marx's beloved proletariat (whom he believed he was saving from oppression) are living in virtual slavery, unable to speak their minds and suffering great physical and financial hardship in places as diverse as Laos and Cuba. Millions of people are dying of starvation in communist North Korea, while its ruler lives in a mansion and attends the symphony.

What happened to Marx and Engel's idealistic notions of a classless society? How did their utopian society turn into one in which the upper class consists of politicians and their enforcers, while everyday people struggle to survive? By failing to take man's baser instincts, such as greed and pride, into consideration, communist countries use Marx's ideas to turn into the very type of society that he fought against.

Basics of Marxism

Marxism is a theory of political and economic thought developed by Karl Marx and Friedrich Engels. Together, these two men spawned a series of rebellions and revolutions that changed the world we live in.

Marx, Engels, and their followers believed that society is dominated by conflicts between the powerful and the subjugated. The Marxists theorized that throughout history the government, the ruling classes, and the capitalists have oppressed the everyday working people, and that it is only through revolution against these rulers that everyone will enjoy true freedom and equality in a classless society.

They believed that the capitalists (those who owned the farms, factories, and shops) made their fortunes by exploiting the people, whom they called the proletariat. In Marx's ideal world, everyone would work hard to better themselves and would cheerfully provide assistance to those who were unable to work.

The Marxists believed that all farms and factories should be owned commonly. This belief in common ownership gave birth to the term "communism" to describe this economic structure. Marx called the idea "economic determinism", because the economic conditions of the people would determine the political and social structures of such a society.

The Marxists also believed that organized religion was one of the tools that governments and the ruling classes (also called the bourgeoisie) used to keep the people, or the proletariat, from thinking for themselves and from being aware, or conscious, that they were being exploited.

Karl Marx and Friedrich Engels

Karl Marx and Friedrich Engels together developed the economic and political theories that would come to be known as Marxism. The two men had many similarities not only in their philosophies, but in their lives as well.

Karl Marx

Karl Heinrich Marx was born on May 5, 1818, in Trier, which was then a part of the Rhineland area of Prussia and is now part of Germany. He was the third of seven children of Heinrich, a lawyer who was descended from a long line of rabbis, and Henrietta, née Pressburg. His parents eventually converted from Judaism to Lutheranism to escape the antisemitism of the Nazis. Marx himself renounced all religion and declared himself an atheist when he was very young.

Marx was home-schooled until the age of 13, when he began attending the Trier Gymnasium. After graduating in 1835, he enrolled in University of Bonn to study law. However, when he received poor grades, probably due to too much socializing, his father made him transfer to the Friedrich-Wilhelms-Universität in Berlin, where he studied philosophy under Georg Wilhelm Friedrich von Hegel.

Hegel's philosophies heavily influenced Marx's theories. Hegel was considered an Idealist; he believed that ideas, thoughts and concepts were the foundations of the world, rather than matter and material things. To the Idealists, material things were only expressions of ideas, especially an "Absolute Idea" or "Universal Spirit". Marx joined a group called the Young Hegelians, who differed somewhat with Hegel and his idea that the material world is founded upon ideas and concepts; they believed that material forces are the basis of reality. This concept of material forces became the basic foundation for all of Marx's later ideas.

After receiving his doctorate in 1841, Marx returned to Berlin intending to teach but gave up the idea when the government began removing radicals from their teaching positions. Instead, he began writing for and eventually became editor-in-chief of an anti-government newspaper called the *Rheinische Zeitung*. It was in Berlin that Marx first met Friedrich Engels, with whom he would later go on to collaborate for the remainder of his life.

In June of 1843, Marx married Jenny von Westphalen, the daughter of a prominent Prussian baron. This enraged not just both families but both communities in which they lived: the noble upper (and ruling) class of the von Westphalens and the Jewish middle class of the Marxes. The match was considered unsuitable because Marx's family was Jewish and Jenny's family was not; because he came from the middle class, though his family was wealthy, and she was not just noble but actually descended from royalty; and because he was four years younger than she was. They married anyway and had seven children, only three of whom survived to adulthood.

Marx moved to Paris in October of 1843 to work with Arnold Ruge, another revolutionary from Germany, on a newspaper called the *Deutsch-Französische Jahrbücher*. After this paper failed, Marx wrote for the *Vorwärts*, one of the most radical German newspapers in Europe, which had was run by a secret society named the League of the Just.

Friedrich Engels

Friedrich Engels was born on November 28, 1820, in Barmen, Prussia, which is now Wuppertal, Germany. He was the eldest of six children of Friedrich, a textile manufacturer and factory owner, and Elisabeth Franziska Mauritia Engels, who were staunch Christians.

Friedrich attended elementary school at Barmen and the Elberfeld gymnasium, which he left at the age of 17. Engels was very athletic and was an expert fencer, swimmer, and horseman. At school he learned several modern and ancient languages and developed an admiration for the ancient Greeks. He also became an expert in the sciences, including biology, chemistry, and physics. He had no further formal schooling, but became a successful businessman, despite his criticism of capitalism, due to pressure from his extremely strict father.

Friedrich became a business apprentice but hated it and left business at the age of 20 in rebellion against his parents' wishes. Engels spent the rest of his life fighting both organized religion and capitalism, even though he, himself, became a factory owner.

Like Marx, Engels was a disciple of Hegel and became a member of the Young Hegelians while performing a year of compulsory military service in Berlin,

After a short period of writing as a freelance journalist, partially using the pseudonym F. Oswald, Engels moved to Manchester, England, in November of 1842 to work as a manager of a textile factory of which his father was part owner. Engels was appalled at the conditions of the workers and what he perceived as their exploitation by the factory owners and wrote a book about it called *The Condition of the Working Class in England.*

Marx and Engels Together

In September of 1844, Engels went to Paris to show Marx his book. The two men immediately saw that they had similar viewpoints and began writing a series of publications including *The Holy Family*.

Engels was considered an expert in military analysis, especially of the role of industry in manufacturing arms. While Marx studied the politics of wars, Engels wrote about their material basis and the origins and nature of armies.

After the *Vorwärts* published an article in 1845 that approved of the assassination attempt on the King of Prussia, Frederick William IV, Marx was deported from France, so he and Engels moved to Belgium. There they formed the Communist Correspondence Committee and continued their joint writing efforts.

In 1848, a period of revolution, rebellion, and upheaval all over Europe, the two men published *The Communist Manifesto* in Belgium. A month after its publication, Belgian authorities arrested Marx and deported both men.

Marx returned to Paris in the midst of the June Days Uprising. When this rebellion failed in 1849, Marx moved to Cologne, Germany, and began publishing the *Neue Rheinische Zeitung*, or *New Rhenish Newspaper*. In Cologne, Marx was twice put on trial, once for a publishing misdemeanor and once for inciting an armed rebellion. He was acquitted both times, but the paper was soon forced to shut down. Marx briefly returned to Paris but was expelled again. Finally, Marx moved to London, where he was to live out the remainder of his life.

During that time, Engels lived in Germany, Belgium, and France, writing and fighting in revolutions, including the 1849 uprisings in Baden and the Palatinate. When these revolutions failed, Engels escaped to Switzerland. In October of 1849, Engels returned to England, where he once again began collaborating with Marx.

Engels could not make any money as a writer in London but he wanted to help support Marx financially, so he returned to his father's textile factory in Manchester. After his father died in 1864, Engels became a partner in the firm. Five years later, he decided that he had enough money to support himself and Marx. He jubilantly sold his share of the company to his partner and moved to London to be near Marx, whom he saw every day.

Meanwhile, Marx had spent a short time working as a correspondent for the New York Herald Tribune while he continued to write. He produced many works, but most of them were not published until after his death.

The Marx family managed to survive on his income from the Tribune articles as well as inheritances from an uncle of Jenny and her mother, who died in 1856, but Engels provided most of their financial support. Still, Marx and his family remained extremely poor and, in 1855, Marx's son Edgar died of tuberculosis.

One of Engels' most important books was *Herr Eugen Dühring's Revolution in Science,* or *Anti-Dühring,* published in 1878.

Jenny died in 1880.

Marx did manage to publish the first volume of his last major work, *Das Kapital*, or *Capital*, but he was in very ill health and died before he was able to complete the remaining two volumes. Marx died of bronchitis and pleurisy at the age of 63 on March 14, 1883, and was buried next to Jenny in London.

After Marx died, Engels completed *Das Kapital* from Marx's notes and spent the rest of his life translating and editing Marx's writings.

In 1884 Engels published *Origins of the Family, Private Property, and the State*, which was one of the earliest feminist books. In it he wrote that marriage was conceived so that men could dominate women, just as the capitalists had dominated their workers.

Engels himself never married but he lived consecutively with two sisters, Mary and Lizzy Burns, fiercely patriotic Irish women who instilled in him a love of the Irish people and support of their class struggle.

Engels died of cancer in London on August 5, 1895.

Chapter 1: Classical Marxism

The main ideas that Marx and Engels proposed are called "classical Marxism" by many people in order to distinguish what the two theorists actually wrote and believed from what later people and governments interpreted them to be or changed them to be in order to suit their own purposes.

These main ideas include the theories of exploitation, alienation, base and superstructure, class consciousness and class struggle, ideology, historical materialism, and political economy.

Exploitation

To explain this theory, Marx wrote that the members of the working class were being exploited by the ruling or capitalist class. In fact, Marx theorized, because the capitalists need the workers to produce goods as cheaply as possible in order to make a profit, the only way for capitalism to thrive, and even to survive, depended on this exploitation. In other words, capitalism can only work if workers are paid less than their work is actually worth.

Alienation

Marx wrote that people were alienated from their true human nature or "Gattungswesen", which is most often translated from the German as "species-essence" or "species-being". He believed that by forcing workers to work for other people and taking away their connection to and ability to profit from their own work, capitalism forces people to become alienated from this essence, even though the workers do not necessarily know or believe that they are alienated.

Base and Superstructure

Marx and Engels used the "base-structure" idea to explain the division of the classes in a capitalist society.

The base includes the philosophical, religious, and other socially conscious ideas. The base determines the superstructure and, after the inevitable revolution, will remain as the basis of the new social organization.

The superstructure includes society's means of production, such as factories and machinery.

Class Consciousness

This idea refers to the awareness that a class has of itself and of the society in which the class lives. The theory includes the ability of a class to act in its own best interests once its members achieve this consciousness. According to Marxism, class consciousness must be achieved in order for the class to stage a revolution successfully.

Ideology

While neither Marx nor Engels ever actually defined this term, Marx used it to describe the image of reality in a society. Engels wrote that it was a thought process that people are conscious of, but described this as a false consciousness. Engels said that people with ideologies are not aware of their true motivations, so they make up imaginary or false ones. Marx believed that, because the ruling class controls the means of production, any ideas and thoughts they have will be made in their own best interests, so their ideologies would also be in their own best interests. Therefore, the driving ideas of the society would be those of the ruling capitalists.

The ideology of a society would, therefore, be extremely important, because it would confuse the alienated group into creating a false consciousness. Marx called one example of such false consciousness "commodity fetishism", which means workers see their labor as capital or as an item that has intrinsic value. To Marx, this degraded the worker and human life by reducing his existence to a commodity that could be bought and sold.

Historical Materialism

Although Marx never actually used the term, "historical materialism", he originated the theory. Marx believed that all history was the history of economic development. To him, this explained how human beings at first worked together to make sure that everyone succeeded until capitalism developed and classes came into being.

Political Economy

The term "political economy" deals with the way that production was organized in young capitalist countries. It describes the methods that human beings use to organize material and distribute the resulting surplus (or deficit). Political economy is the study of the means of production, especially capital, and how this shows up in the economy.

Chapter 2: The Young Hegelians

When Marx was a student at the University of Bonn, he met a group of followers of the recently deceased German philosopher Georg Wilhelm Friedrich (G. W. F.) Hegel (1770–1831).

G. W. F. Hegel

Hegel was an idealist who developed a method of thesis (developing or inventing an idea), antithesis (testing it by seeing if the opposite was true), and synthesis (reasoning logically), called a "dialectic", that he believed was best used to analyze ideas to form a new theory.

Hegel and his followers believed that reason (or logic) and freedom were the most important forces in history and that the human spirit could overcome irrationality and all of the similar opposing forces. Hegel actually wrote that reason and freedom had gone as far as they could go and achieved perfection in the Prussian government and that the time in which he was living was the end of history. This, of course, could not have been further from the truth. Even at that time, the governments of France, Great Britain, and the United States had achieved much higher levels of freedom for their citizens.

The Right Hegelians

There were two groups of Hegel's followers. The Right, or Old, Hegelians believed the same thing that Hegel did. They were certain that Hegel's dialectical method could be used to explain all of reality. This group was made up of slightly more conservative people such as university professors. Like Hegel, these followers were orthodox in their religious beliefs and conformist in their political beliefs.

The Young Hegelians

The group to which Marx and Engels belonged, the Young Hegelians, was composed of the more radically leftist members. These young people thought that Hegel's theory of the end of history conflicted with other aspects of his philosophy. They saw that the dialectic could not possibly be complete, considering the religious beliefs and the lack of religious and political freedom in Prussian society.

The Young Hegelians re-interpreted Hegel's methods and used them to try to prove that religious leaders were the primary ruling class and needed to be rebelled against.

Marx vs. the Young Hegelians

In the beginning, Marx was sympathetic with the Young Hegelians and their method of attacking the Christian church to try to undermine the Prussian government. However, he eventually decided that the real ruling class was composed of the capitalists and business- and landowners, who used religion as a shield to hide behind so that the people would not be able to see where the real power lay. This is where his famous "opium of the people" line came into play. Marx then parted ways with the Young Hegelians over these religious theories, even writing a work called *The German Ideology* to dispute them.

While Marx came to disagree with both Hegel and the Young Hegelians, he did admit that he was influenced by Hegel's method of analyzing events (dialectics) and used it to criticize economics, politics, religion, and authority.

Bruno Bauer

One of the more radical members of the group was Bruno Bauer, with whom Marx became good friends. In July 1841, the two scandalized their schoolmates by getting drunk and riding through the street on donkeys. The friendship ended for good after Marx met Engels in Paris in 1844 and the pair wrote a criticism of Bauer's philosophies and writings called *Die Heilige Familie* (*The Holy Family*), which was published in 1845.

Engels vs. the Young Hegelians

Engels was also a member of the Young Hegelians. He and Marx created their view of socialism and developed an analysis of history based on materialism, which is now called historical materialism. He and Marx famously criticized the Young Hegelians and Ludwig Feuerbach in two of the books that they wrote together, *The Holy Family* and *The German Ideology*. The most important theory of their materialist view of history is that "social being precedes social consciousness." In other words, a person can become socially conscious only after experiencing society firsthand.

Other Young Hegelians

Marx was also influenced by some of the ideas of some of the other members of the Young Hegelians. A brief discussion of some of them follows.

Ludwig Feuerbach

While Marx was working in France as a journalist at *Vorwärts!* (*Forward!*), a German-language newspaper for expatriate radicals, he continued to write about his ideas of socialism that were based on Hegel's and Feuerbach's views on materialism, while at the same time criticizing other European liberals and socialists. In 1845, the French government finally shut down the newspaper and kicked Marx out of the country. Eventually, Marx abandoned Feuerbach's philosophies, as well.

Max Stirner

Although Max Stirner socialized with the Young Hegelians every now and then, he disagreed vehemently with the group members. He even wrote a devastating satire of them work, *Der Einzige und Sein Eigentum*, or *The Ego and Its Own*.

Arnold Ruge

As an advocate of a free and united Germany, Arnold Ruge believed in Hegel's philosophy that history was a progression towards freedom. He also subscribed to Hegel's theory of the rational general will. However, he did not like Hegel's idea that there would be no future history, because that theory did not allow for any innovation and change.

Edgar Bauer

Probably the most radical of the group was Edgar Bauer, the younger brother of Bruno Bauer. Some of his early writings actually tried to justify political terrorism.

Karl Schmidt

Karl Schmidt was the last Young Hegelian. He described the history of the Hegelians in his work *The Realm of Understanding and the Individual* and came to the final realization that "I am only myself."

The Price They Paid

This radical thinking cost many of the Young Hegelians dearly. Karl Neuwerck (another member of the group) and Bruno Bauer were fired from their teaching positions. Marx and some of the other group members were told not to submit their dissertations to the University of Berlin, because their radical reputations would prevent the papers from being accepted. Marx eventually had his dissertation accepted by the University of Jena, earning him a PhD.

Chapter 3: Marx's Theory of Human Nature and Alienation

Marx believed that a capitalist society forced people to be alienated, or separated, from their basic human nature. "Entfremdung", which means "estrangement" in German, is the word Marx used to describe this alienation. The word is used to describe things that belong together naturally but are separated; it is also used for things that should be harmonious but are in discord.

Although they were written in 1844, Marx's notes on his viewpoint of human nature and what came to be known as his theory of alienation were not found or published until the 20th century, well after his death. This study was called *Economic and Philosophical Manuscripts of 1844*.

Human Nature

Marx believed that it was a part of human nature to want fulfilling work that creates something of value both to society as well as to the person who created it. He believed that when people worked for themselves in careers such as as craftsman, artisan, or farmer, for which they received the full payment or value of the items they produced with their own labor, they were happy and fulfilled.

Development of Alienation

As the Middle Ages ended and the Industrial Revolution began, people stopped working for themselves making and selling their own products and began working for other people in factories and businesses owned by others, whom Marx called capitalists or the bourgeoisie. When this movement happened, workers (called the proletariat) began to move away from their basic human natures, making them feel unfulfilled and alienated.

Four Types of Alienation

Marx described four main types of alienation for workers in an industrial society.

Alienation from the End Product

The first type is alienation from the goods they produce. The workers themselves do not feel as if they have any stake in their goods because they design neither the product nor the manufacturing process. They have no pride in their work because they feel as if they are just an extension of the means of production that their capitalist bosses own. The workers are paid as low a wage as possible so the bosses can increase their profits, none of which go to the people who actually produce any tangible goods.

Alienation from the Work Process

The second point of alienation is alienation from the actual process of working. Because the worker has no control over this process, he feels powerless. This is especially true of assembly line work, which is repetitive, isolating, and boring. It is particularly true when a worker is making only a small part of a larger object, especially if it is a large object that the worker cannot afford to purchase himself, such as a motor of an airplane or part of a yacht. This means the worker does not care about the quality of the work he produces, only the wage that he earns for producing it.

Alienation from the True Self

The third point of alienation that Marx described was alienation from the worker's true self, which Marx called "species-being". This theory describes the social alienation of people from their true natures. The German word that Marx used to describe this true human nature was "Gattungswesen", which translates to either "species essence" or "species being". Marx believed that it was human nature to be free and productive. He also believed that capitalism and its exploitation of the proletariat destroyed this freedom and, therefore, caused people to spend their lives disoriented and separated from their true characters.

He described two parts of species essence. The first is known as "plurality". Marx believed that it is human nature to want to do more than one activity at a time. The second part is known as "dynamism". Marx used this term to describe the fact that, unlike animals, people are able to conceive of the result of their activities. In a capitalist society, workers who spend all of their days, and even years, working to manufacture a small part of a car or other machine are completely separated from the end product of their labor.

Alienation from Other People

The fourth and final point that Marx made was the alienation of workers from other people. Instead of being involved in a community that is working towards a common goal of either bettering their positions or surviving, industrial workers are pitted against one another to compete for better wages or better work. Capitalism also pits workers against business owners because business owners try to get as much labor as possible out of their workers, while workers try to get better wages and working conditions.

Alienation of the Capitalists

Marx theorized that the business owners and other capitalists were also alienated. He believed, however, that they relished this alienation, because it gave them a feeling of strength, power, and control over their workers.

Religion's Role in Alienation

Marx drew a great deal of his alienation theory from the writings of two fellow members of the Young Hegelians, Feuerbach's *The Essence of Christianity* and Stirner's *The Ego and Its Own*.

Feuerbach wrote that the idea of a God alienated people from their own human characteristics. Marx took this a step further with his "opiate of the masses" statement, insisting that religion had a major role in the alienation process.

There were three reasons for or causes of this alienation. The first way that religion alienated people from their true selves was that religion stopped people from seeking to better themselves and achieve their own highest potential of perfection, because only God is perfect. The second cause was that religion removed people's desire for wanting to live their best lives because any of their mistakes or bad behavior would be forgiven in the afterlife. The third cause was that religion had the result of stopping people from striving to achieve more on earth, because they would be rewarded by a beautiful (albeit mythical) afterlife.

Stirner wrote that the idea of humanity in general is alienating for individuals, because they are just a small cog in a very large machine, or, as Star Trek's Mr. Spock would put it, "The needs of the many outweigh the needs of the few."

Marx and Engels' response to these works came in their work, "The German Ideology".

Triumph Over Alienation

Marx wrote that in order for people to be truly happy in life, they need to overcome this alienation and realize their true selves. He called this activity self-actualization. However, he believed that before this self-actualization took place, the proletariat would have been so taken advantage of and impoverished by the capitalists that they would revolt just to be able to survive economically.

Chapter 4: Marx's Economic Theory of History

Marx believed that all history could be traced back to economic and class conflicts. His idealism is apparent in the stages of economic development that he identifies, at least in Western civilizations, as follows.

Stage 1: Primitive Communism

According to Marx, primitive communism is the natural state of tribal societies. As in the saying "It takes a village to raise a child," in a primitive society, everyone works for the common good, no one person has more than any other, and people pool their resources so that nobody goes hungry and everyone's physical needs are met.

As anyone who has ever lived in or read about such a society knows, this is an extremely, almost ridiculously, idealistic view of human nature. In any real society, there are people who are lazy and take advantage of the hard work of others, and there are hard-working people who resent being taken advantage of. There are also greedy people who demand more than their fair share of material goods, while there are those who are either so meek or so intimidated that they give in to these bullies.

Stage 2: Slave Society

Marx described the second stage of development as a city-state, such as the ones in ancient Egypt, Rome, and Greece. This stage also includes development of the aristocracy, with those who are smarter (or at least stronger and greedier) enslaving the weaker.

Stage 3: Feudalism

In the feudal stage, aristocrats become the undisputed ruling class and continue to exploit the slaves or serfs. During this stage, capitalism develops when merchants sell their wares for profit. This was the case in medieval Europe when kings and lords forced servitude and taxes upon those they ruled.

Stage 4: Capitalism

In Marx's fourth stage of economic development, capitalists take over as the ruling class (bourgeoisie). They create the proletariat (working class) when they begin employing workers to do their production for them. This is the stage that took place during the Industrial Revolution.

Stage 5: Socialism

During socialism, according to Marx, the workers become conscious of the exploitation of their own class, stage a proletarian revolution against their capitalist exploiters, and take over as the rulers. In Marx's romantic, idealized vision of humanity, the new ruling (working) class will then create a perfect socialist society in which all people are equal and material goods are freely and evenly distributed to all who need them. The closest the world ever came to this stage in reality would probably be the "honeymoon" periods that immediately followed the workers' revolutions in countries such as Russia and Cuba, when Lenin and Castro rewarded those who had fought with them.

Stage 6: Communism

In Marx's ideal world, the result of the revolution is a classless, stateless society known as communism. To Marx, a communist state such as China would be an oxymoron. This contradiction has led people to call Marx's original theories classical Marxism. His concept of communism is a far cry from the real-world communist states that were created by the proletarian revolutions that took place in countries such as the North Korea and Cuba. In those communist states, the new ruling class crushes every form of free speech by shipping dissenters off to labor camps or political prisons, and people stand in line for hours just to buy a carelessly made pair of shoes or an overpriced sack of flour.

Chapter 5: Marx's Theory of Value and Surplus Value

Marxism started out as an economic theory, rather than a political system. Marx and Engels were mainly concerned with ending the exploitation of workers. The only reason that the two men wrote anything about the government of a country was that they believed that it was the capitalists, the exploiters of the workers, who really controlled the government, even if it was from behind the scenes.

Because Marxism is really an economic system, the theories of value and surplus value are two of the most important ideas and are central to Marxist philosophy.

According to Marx, value refers to the amount of labor that it takes to make an item. In order for capitalism to work, the business owner must make a profit. In order to make a profit, he must charge more for the items that his workers produce than he pays them to produce the items. The business owner pockets the difference in profits. Marx called the difference between what the workers earn to produce an item and what the item sells for "surplus value". Contributing to this surplus value is the amount of time the workers spend at work after they have already earned what they need to survive. Marx wrote that this was exploitation of the worker, taking advantage of him and usurping the value of his labor for the business owner's advancement.

For example, let's imagine that an owner has a factory that can produce 100 units a day. He has two workers that he pays, say, $10 an hour. Each person works 8 hours per day and makes 80 units per day. Each unit takes six minutes to make, which means that each unit contains a labor value of six minutes. The two workers combined make 160 units and are paid $160, total. The owner sells the 160 units for $10 each, for a total of $1,600. The difference between the $1,600 that the items sell for and the $160 that the workers are paid for making them is $1,440. The $1,440 of profit is what Marx called surplus value. Of course, the owner must also pay taxes and other costs of doing business, but these do not directly contribute to the exploitation of the workers, so these items are not included when the surplus value is measured.

Exploitation of the Worker by the Capitalists

In ancient and medieval times, people and slaves were forced by their rulers to work for them using physical means such as chains, starvation, and even beatings.

In capitalist societies, workers are exploited by more subtle methods. People who do not own any means of production themselves must go to work for others who do have a means of production. This relationship is supposedly voluntary, because the worker gets to choose his boss or business. However, in reality, the worker basically has no choice, because he needs to work in order to eat and to provide shelter and clothing for himself and the members of his family. This lack of choice as to whether to work for another, according to Marx and Engels, meant that this relationship by its very nature has to result in the business owner exploiting the worker.

Factory machines cannot produce anything by themselves; they need workers to operate them, so the owners, who produce nothing of value by themselves, make all of their profits from the workers. Because the workers must work to survive, they have to continue to make themselves available for exploitation.

Additionally, according to Marx, the class that controls the material things in society also controls its ideas. Because the capitalists control the means of production, they are the ruling class that also controls society. This means that the society does what is in the best interests of the ruling class, so the society does what the capitalists want. Eventually, Marx wrote, the working class of proletarians would realize that they are being exploited and controlled by their capitalist bosses and would revolt against this exploitation.

Revolution of the Exploited Proletariat

Marx also theorized that capitalism is an antagonistic relationship, with the two sides never able to compromise and with one side always being taken advantage of by the other. As soon as the workers (the proletariat) had their consciousness raised (by the Marxists, of course), they would realize how much they were being exploited by the business owners (also called capitalists or bourgeoisie), Marx believed, the proletariat would revolt.

Marx believed that both the capitalist system as well as the bourgeoisie were full of contradictions and faults that would increase as industrialization advanced. The system would face severe economic downturns and eventual crises. As Marx and Engels wrote in *The Communist Manifesto*, the first successful revolution of the proletariat would take place in a highly industrialized country in which the workers' consciousness was very advanced.

Of course, Marx and the Marxists believed it was their job to speed up this revolution by raising workers' consciousness to the fact that they were being exploited. They did this by unionizing workers all over the world and by supporting any political organization that favored these labor unions.

After the Revolution

Once the revolution succeeded, according to Marx, the proletariat would become the ruling class. They would then place all of the means of production in the hands of the state, which would be controlled by all of the workers collectively. Production would increase quickly. There would be no more classes, because the means of production would be owned by everyone, not by any particular group.

The state, which had previously controlled the economy and oppressed and took advantage of the workers, would then be replaced by a model system of economic and social cooperation. Bourgeois institutions such as the church and family, which had gone along with the state in its exploitation of the worker, would magically disappear, and everyone would find their true nature and be completely fulfilled. And everyone would live happily ever after.

Chapter 6: The Proletariat and the Working Class

The word "proletariat" comes from the Latin word "proletarius", which means a citizen of the lowest class. The root of this word is "proli", which means "offspring". In the Roman census, people who had no property had their children, or "proli", listed as their property, so the word proletarius originally referred to landless freemen who had no property other than their children. They had been forced out of the labor market by the institution of slavery and became parasites on society, bleeding it of valuable resources without making any concrete contributions to it.

Creation of the Proletariat

When Marx used the word proletariat, he was referring only to people who worked in industrial production such as factory workers. He applied the term "working class" to include everyone who was forced to work for a living. Both terms were used to refer especially to those people who have little or no property and no way to produce property or wealth.

As Marx saw it, any historical progress has been advanced by the conflict between economic classes. Engels wrote in *The Principles of Communism* that, while the working class and the working poor had always existed, it was only after the feudal system broke up that the proletariat came into being. When serfs and peasant farmers began to assert their rights from the feudal lords, they began to become small shopowners and traders. Many of these owners formed guilds and started hiring workers to help them create wealth. This created capitalism and thus the proletariat.

When society developed into this capitalist system, this new class of dispossessed serfs and peasants, who had no lands or property, came into being. When people were forced to sell their hard work for wages in the new industrial centers, the robber barons of the 19th century's Industrial Revolution began to take terrible advantage of them, and the class struggle took off.

Conflict of Interest

In Marxism, the proletariat and the capitalists, or "bourgeoisie", are polar opposites, because workers always want their wages to increase while the owners need the wages to be as low as possible. Marx called this class struggle the "materialist dialectic". The proletariat are, by necessity, by far the larger class—but, according to Marx, the bourgeoisie not only own most of the wealth, they also control the government, military, and religious organizations.

In addition to these two groups, there are also the petite bourgeoisie, who are self-employed, and the, "lumpen proletariat" or "rag-proletariat", such as pickpockets, beggars, prostitutes, and con artists, who are illegally employed. While Marx considered the lumpen proletariat to be a burden on society, many other socialists struggle with the decision of whether to include them with the wage-earning members of the proletariat when they try to get organized and whether to try to represent them in their negotiations.

Some people refer to proletarians as people who receive wages, while those who receive salaries are called the "salariat". Marx, however, did not make this distinction; he believed that anyone who performed work from which another person profited was a member of the proletariat. He also believed that the way to determine whether a person was a member of the proletariat or a member of the bourgeoisie was to see which side she or he joined during a strike.

These differences result in what Marx called the class struggle and affect both sides with unionizing, strikes, and lockouts.

Exploitation of the Proletariat

According to Marx, the only way for a capitalist society to survive was to exploit the proletariat.

Marx's theory states that the exploitation follows this procedure. The workers are too poor to own any means of production, so they must use other people's means of production to produce goods so they can earn money to live. Rather than pay to use those means of production, they hire themselves out to other people to work for them and they actually become their employer's means of production. This is because the employer sells the goods that the worker produces.

Only a small part of the money goes to the worker's salary. This is called a variable expense.

Another small part goes towards renewing and keeping up the means of production. This is the constant expense.

The last portion is what Marx called the "surplus value". Part of it goes to pay rent, taxes, and other costs of doing business, while part of it is the business owner's profit.

Marx and the Marxists believe that any surplus value exploits workers by using them to increase the wealth of the business owner without fairly compensating the workers.

If Marx were alive today, he would undoubtedly point to the "Occupy" movement of the self-described 99% as proof that capitalism does not work and that people will always ultimately revolt against a system that they see as exploiting them.

Revolution of the Proletariat

According to Marxist principles, capitalism was born from this class struggle, and socialism or communism will be born from it as well.

Marx urged the proletariat to rebel against this exploitation and replace the capitalist system with what he called a dictatorship of the proletariat. This period would be a transition between the old system and a new system in which nobody would be able to exploit anyone else. In order to do this, the proletariat would need to get rid of the class system and all of the existing relationships between the proletariat and the bourgeoisie.

After the transitional period, the people would form a new communist society, in which all people would collectively own all means of production and property. According to Marx's idealistic views, everyone would work to ensure that everyone else was free, and nobody would be greedy or want or take more than they were entitled to.

In reality, when the communists came in to power in the Soviet Union, China, Cuba, and other countries, power was actually taken away from the proletariat and placed in the hands of central committee members who ended up being the new ruling class.

Chapter 7: Class Struggle and False Consciousness

Marx called his theory "scientific socialism" and claimed that it was based on science.

In Marx's theories of value and alienation, he stated that throughout history, an ongoing struggle took place between two classes: the bourgeoisie who own the means of production, such as factories and machinery, and the proletariat, who work for wages.

Marx claimed that he had a revelation about the laws of history that revealed the necessity for this class struggle. He predicted that most capitalists would eventually go bankrupt from fierce competition, leaving a few monopolies that controlled the production of almost all goods. To Marx, this was one of the great contradictions of capitalism. Rather than creating better products at lower costs, it would create monopolies that exploited both workers and consumers.

The former capitalists would then be forced to become members of the proletariat, which would make the labor supply larger, resulting in lower wages and creating what Marx referred to as a "reserve army of the unemployed".

Marx also believed that the chaotic nature of market economies ends up creating an economic crisis as supply and demand become unequal, eventually resulting in severe depressions. He believed that advanced capitalist economies were especially prone to these conflicts, finally destroying themselves completely, after which the proletariat will suddenly realize it has the power to overthrow the few remaining capitalists and the entire system.

Dialectic Materialism

A dialectic is an argument among classes or groups. Each class has its own interests and needs. "Dialectical materialism" is Marx's idea that human history is the history of class conflicts. Different classes conflict with each other, eventually resulting in social change.

Marxists believe that rebellions and revolutions in which the proletariat (workers) fight and overthrow the capitalists are not only inevitable, they are necessary.

After the proletariat wins, they will set up a socialist "workers' state", a government in which the workers themselves rule. According to Marx, this is a temporary state that will eventually be replaced by a communist state, a classless society in which the capitalists are abolished and the workers own all of the means of production.

False Consciousness

Class consciousness refers to the awareness of the worker to his plight. It also describes a class's capability of acting in a rational manner in its own best interests; therefore, a workers must achieve class consciousness in order to perform a successful revolution.

Marx and Engels use the term "false consciousness" to describe the views that the workers have of their own situation that are given to them or influenced by the ruling capitalist class, which includes the church and government that it controls.

The primary goal of a Leninist movement is to educate and enlighten the proletariat to remove the false consciousness that the bourgeoisie has instilled in the workers in order to make them more compliant, docile, and easier to exploit. After the proletariat has achieved true class consciousness, the party will coordinate their revolution.

Chapter 8: Marx and Religion

Although the Marx family was originally Jewish, they converted to Lutheranism in an effort to avoid religious prejudice and the increasing number and effect of German laws that prevented Jews from holding many positions, such as teaching in schools and holding office. It was this discrimination that led young Marx to the conclusion that religion was just a device that the government used to destroy people's lives, seemingly on a whim. Even though he was very young, after he saw the way the government was using religion as an excuse to discriminate against Jews and other sects, Marx declared himself an atheist.

Marx derived much of his later ideas about religion from Moses Hess, who was a fellow member of the Young Hegelians. Although Marx and Hess did not agree in the long run, Marx developed his theory of the relationship between religion, society, and the government from their talks on the topic.

Engels and Religion

Engels also hated religion, but he had more personal reasons. His parents were religious fanatics who called themselves devout Christians. Engels' father, who was also named Friedrich, was also extremely strict, tyrannical, and cruel to his children, particularly his eldest son and namesake. Engels came to hate his father and everything associated with him, especially business and religion. Like Marx, Engels believed that religion was a tool of repression and oppression. He tried to persuade working-class people that they would never be truly free and equal if they did not remove the oppressive church from their lives.

Religion as a Tool of the State's Oppression

Marx thoroughly rejected religion and the organizations that upheld it as tools that governments used to oppress working people, keeping them from thinking for themselves. He believed that religion not only kept the workers oppressed, it also kept them unaware of their own exploitation.

Because civil governments and businesses were often closely associated with the local religious institutions, they promised people a better life if they "behaved" themselves and did what they were told, in the eyes of Marx and Engels. The two men believed that this led people into virtual slavery. If they dared to protest their situation, they weren't being "good" Christians (all of Europe was Christian at that point) and would be punished severely in the afterlife. By striking these fears into their members, religious organizations were able to keep them quiet and subservient.

Marx also believed that religious organizations acted hypocritically, preaching about love and living a simple life while themselves forming alliances with oppressive governments and stealing jewels, gold, and other precious metals to use on their altars and in their places of worship.

Denying Our Best Selves

Marx also disliked religion because he believed it prevented people from being their best selves. Projecting our ideals onto a strange, unknowable creature called a god, Marx believed, alienates us from our higher purposes and aspirations. By making us believe that only God is perfect, religion automatically makes us believe that we cannot aspire to reach the highest levels of conduct and achievement.

Marx wrote "The holy form of human self-estrangement has been unmasked", meaning that religion forces us to deny our true selves. That is, it strips us of our dignity by forcing us to kowtow to religious leaders who would deny us our right to protest against our oppression.

Opium of the People

Marx's most famous saying about religion is often misunderstood and misquoted. The actual quotation from "About the Attitude of the Working Party Toward the Religion" is "Religion is the sigh of the oppressed creature, the heart of a heartless world, and the soul of soulless conditions. It is the opium of the people." This means that religion is used to artificially soothe people who are confused and lost and thus gives them false hope. According to Marx, religion keeps people blissfully unaware of their own state of oppression in the same way that a drug addict is completely focused only on finding another "fix."

Like opium, Marx felt, religion does not cure any illness or disease; it simply masks the pain that people feel in their everyday existence. Moreover, religion, like opium, helps people to forget the reasons that they are suffering. It makes them envision an imaginary afterlife in which their pain will magically stop, so they do not bother to try to stop it now by rising up against their circumstances and oppressors. What is worse, this "drug" is administered by the very same oppressors who are responsible for this pain.

Marx continued, "The abolition of religion as the illusory happiness of the people is required for their real happiness," believing that religion keeps people from achieving true happiness in life and that in order to find happiness, working-class people need to become aware of their own oppression.

Religion in Communist Countries

Even today, most communist countries prohibit or severely limit the church's influence. Those who attend church services are mostly older people. Younger people either bought into the communists' theory of oppression or pretended to do so, because they were afraid of being viewed by the government as a nonconformist at best or even as a rebel.

Ironically, by discouraging people from participating in religious services—which had the same basic effect as forbidding it—these governments oppressed their people just as much as governments who discriminated against a particular sect.

But people in all countries still looked to a higher power and many still attended church services, either openly or secretly. After the break-up of the Soviet Union, some of the first scenes broadcast to the outside world showed thousands of former Soviet citizens freely and joyfully attending services in the newly-reopened Orthodox churches.

Chapter 9: Schools and Societies of Marxist Thinkers and Researchers

Marxism has many forms and interpretations. Any political theory or any government that is based even loosely on Marx's and Engels' writings can be called Marxism. Many researchers also take a Marxist approach to their work in such fields as history, economics, literature, anthropology, art, and drama.

Traits Common to Marxist Societies

Most Marxists have the following beliefs in common:

- Capitalist societies are built on the exploitation of workers by people who own the capital.

- History is based on the struggle between these two classes.

- What determines which class a person belongs to is whether he is an owner of capital or works for wages.

- Social relations between the classes are affected by material conditions and affect the society's history.

- Eventually the dialectical process (class conflict) and the workers' increasing consciousness of their exploitation will result in a revolution that will replace the class system with a classless society in which all citizens will jointly hold all means of production.

Points of Disagreement

One of the main points of disagreement between Marxists is how much they believe in the proletarian revolution as a way for people to become free and enlightened. Another area is how a revolution should occur, and how much of a chance it has to succeed.

Marxism is a variety of socialism, but many Marxists believe that there has never been a government who actually followed pure Marxist principles, while others believe that it is not possible to achieve such a government as we know.

Schools of Marxist Thinkers

There are many different schools and forms of Marxist thinkers. Some schools currently have state governments based on their ideas, while governments based on other ideas have proven unsuccessful.

Structural Marxism

Structural Marxism is based on structural theory and the work of French philosopher Louis Althusser and his followers. It became popular in France during the 1960s and 70s and spread beyond France around the late 1970s.

Marxist Humanism

Marxist humanism is based mostly on Marx's earlier writings, particularly his *Economic and Philosophical Manuscripts of 1844*, in which he presents his theory of alienation. Marxist Humanists believe that in order to understand Marx's later works, people need to understand the ideas in his earlier writings.

Marxist humanists believe that mainstream Marxism developed unevenly because Marx's earlier writings were not discovered until his later works were already popular. For example, the 1844 manuscripts were not found until long after Marx's death and were not published until 1932.

Louis Althusser considered Marxist humanism a revisionist branch and created an opposing, "antihumanism" movement.

Western Marxism

Western Marxism is a variety of Marxism whose proponents are based in western Europe,cCentral Europe, and North America. These theorists hold different beliefs from those in China, the former Soviet Union, and other countries in the Eastern Bloc.

Neo-Marxism

Neo-Marxism is based on the earliest writings of Marx, before he became associated with Engels. Those writings focused more on idealism than materialism, so the Neo-Marxists are more libertarian and believe in Max Weber's theories that classes are based on social inequality, rather than just material status.

Cultural Marxism

Cultural Marxism analyzes the place of art, literature, drama, and the media in a society, and emphasizes conflicts between the sexes and races in addition to the conflicts between economic classes. Cultural Marxism grew in popularity in the 1920s and was the form used by the Frankfurt School and people at the Centre for Contemporary Cultural Studies in Birmingham, England.

The Frankfurt School

The Frankfurt School is a school of Neo-Marxists who were philosophers, social researchers, and social theorists. The group got its start at Germany's Institute for Social Research (Institut für Sozialforschung) at the University of Frankfurt am Main in Germany. It was originally composed of Marxist dissenters who were adamantly opposed to capitalism. These critics believed that some of Marx's followers had actually focused narrowly on a small part of Marx's ideas and used them to defend communism and social democrats.

The members of the Frankfurt School were influenced by the failed revolutions in Europe after World War I and the appearance of the Nazi party in Germany, which had a thriving economy as well as a flourishing cultural scene and advanced technology. These theorists tried to determine how Marx had missed the conditions that led to these movements and filled in his omissions with ideas from other theorists.

Max Weber and Sigmund Freud were both major influences on this movement.

Autonomist Marxism

Autonomist Marxism can be applied to several social movements throughout the world where networks are structured autonomously or horizontally rather than in a hierarchy, such as in a union or political party. Autonomist Marxists believe that the working classes in advanced capitalist countries are the main force of change in building capital.

One Autonomist Marxist was Harry Cleaver, who expanded the definition of "worker" to include those who did salaried work (such as skilled professionals like doctors and teachers) as well as unpaid workers (such as homemakers).

More recent Autonomist Marxist philosophers include Michael Hardt and Antonio Negri, who believe that the best way to fight the "neoliberal regime" of accumulating capital is to organize networks to oppose them. These theorists predict that there will be a huge change in the dynamics of capital accumulation that will form a new empire in the 21st century.

Analytical Marxism

Analytical Marxism is associated mostly with a group of English and English-speaking theorists and social scientists called the September Group, so named because they meet every other September. They also called their theories "non-bullshit Marxism". This group was formed during the 1980s with a mission of trying to clarify ideas that are often foggy and complicated.

Chapter 10: Marxism Around the World

There have been, and still are, several state governments around the world that are based on Marxist principles. While there are other socialist governments in several countries around the world, many of those western governments, such as Sweden's, have disavowed any links to Marx or his theories.

Some countries that consider themselves Marxist or socialist are actually communist or have governments that have corrupted Marxist theories. These include Vietnam, Cuba, and China. Venezuela also has a form of socialist government. Of all these countries, only Laos and Cuba still keep a strong control over the country's means of production.

While many people consider it a corruption of Marx's theories, communism is also loosely based on Marxism. The main difference between Marxism and communism is that Marxism is a framework based on a theory of the economic differences between workers and capitalists, Communism tries to establish a society in which all means of production, as well as the goods they produce, are communally named by everyone. There are many people who share Marxist beliefs who are not in favor of communism.

Countries that follow Marxist principles but are ruled by communist parties would be considered oxymorons by Marx. He reserved that term for the classless society that would take place after the wealth had been distributed to all and the means of production were communally owned by all members of the state.

Marxism-Leninism

Marxism-Leninism refers to the version of Marxism developed by Vladimir Lenin after the Russian Revolution. Other political groups, however, have used this term describe their own philosophies and ideologies.

The basic ideas of Marxism-Leninism are a belief that the only way to successfully defeat capitalism is by violent revolution, followed by the dictatorship of the proletariat, which would be the first step in the movement towards true communism. Lenin also believed that there had to be a ruling party to guide the proletariat in their journey. This school follows the teachings of both Marx and Engels as well as those of Lenin and, later, Joseph Stalin.

People who subscribe to this theory differ as to who would be the best person to uphold these principles. Some of these people follow China's Mao Zedong and are called Maoists, while others, such as the Hoxhaites, renounce Mao.

The primary goal of the Leninists is to raise the class consciousness of the proletariat and remove their false consciousness, such as religion and nationalism. After the proletariat gains this class consciousness, the party will lead the proletariat in overthrowing the existing government and seizing control of the means of production as well as political and economic power.

Finally, the workers will start their own "dictatorship of the proletariat", which will have absolute control of the nation. The state will be government by direct democracy of the proletariat, with workers wielding power through local councils called "soviets". This will lead to socialism. The entire proletariat will be revolutionaries and the party will dissolve, since it will no longer be needed.

Trotskyism

Trotskyism is the form of Marxism advocated by Leon Trotsky, a Bolshevik-Leninist. Trotsky wanted to establish a leading party. He considered himself an orthodox Marxist. Trotsky's political views differed sharply from those of Stalin, primarily in the desire for a "permanent revolution". There are still many groups that subscribe to this belief.

Trotsky's theory of "permanent revolution" stated that in those countries that had not yet had a successful bourgeois-democratic revolution, the proletariat needed to carry out an ongoing socialist or communist revolution.

Trotsky also believed that socialist countries would not be able to withstand pressure from capitalist countries on their own, so there needed to take place a series of quick revolutions all over the capitalist world, especially in countries with well-developed industries and proletariats. Trotskyists actually claim to support democracy while at the same time opposing imperialism and advocating the spread of worldwide revolutions.

Trotsky theorized that the Russian state was controlled by a bureaucracy whose interests were opposed to those of the proletariat. He called for an internal revolution to restore social democracy in the Soviet Union. He believed that if the people did not remove the Stalinists from power, the bureaucracy would eventually revert to capitalism and exploit the workers once again. Many Trotskyists believe that that is exactly what happened after the breakup of the Soviet Union.

Maoism

Maoism is a variety of Marxism-Leninism that is based on the teachings of Chinese communist leader Mao Zedong.

The term "Mao Zedong thought" is the term used by the Communist Party of China. The word "Maoism" is never used in China except as a pejorative. In the same manner, Maoist groups outside of China usually call themselves Marxist-Leninist, which supports Mao's opinion that he did not change Marxism-Leninism but developed it further. Other Maoist groups believe that Mao's theories have made significant contributions additions to Marxist theory, so they call themselves "Marxist-Leninist-Maoists" or just "Maoists".

Since the beginning of the current Chinese market economy reforms, the official role of Mao's ideology has been radically changed and significantly reduced.

One of Mao's primary beliefs was that the peasants of the countryside should be a driving force behind the revolution of the proletariat and become main members of the subsequent ruling Communist party. These peasants played a leading role in bringing the Communist Party into power in China in the People's War of the 1920s and 30s.

Maoism also differed from Marxism-Leninism in making a priority of rural development rather than industrial development. Mao believed that, in a country in which a majority of people were peasants, the focus needed to be on bringing these peasants into socialism.

Maoism has a strict military strategy and doctrine, as illustrated by Mao's quotation, "Political power grows from the barrel of the gun."

When the Soviet Union collapsed, China adopted many free-market economy ideas, calling them a development of Marxism rather than a rejection of it.

Belarus

The agricultural policy of Belarus follows communist principles, while its economy has been called "market socialism". The country's president, Alexander Lukashenko, is also an admirer of the former Soviet Union government.

North Korea

The official ideology of the Korean Workers' Party, led by Chairman Kim Jong-il, is called "Juche". While it does not officially follow Marxist-Leninist principles as in the Soviet Union, it is supposedly a form of communism, but it is also a hard-line dictatorship.

Libya

Libya was considered a socialist country until its recent rebellion. The recently-deposed (and late) leader Colonel Muammar al-Gaddafi had strong ties with the former Soviet Union as well as other Eastern Bloc and communist countries. Gaddafi described the country's official ideology as Islamic socialism.

United Kingdom

The Labour Party of Great Britain once described itself as a socialist political party. The party belongs to an organization called Socialist International, which was established by members of trade unions and revolutionary and reformist socialist parties such as the socialist Fabian Society and the Social Democratic Federation.

Vietnam

After the reunification of the country, Vietnam actually began to move away from the communist theories of the former North Vietnam and has recently begun a wave of privatization of its factories and other means of production.

Cuba

The government of Fidel Castro's Cuba follows Marxist communist principles and is likely to continue doing so if and when his brother succeeds the elderly leader, who is reportedly being treated for cancer.

Chapter 11: Criticisms

There are so many criticisms of Marxism that it is difficult to limit them to just a few. Some of these criticisms are regarding Marx's theories, while others are more concerned with their interpretations and use.

Theory of Value

Marx's labor theory of value has been discounted by modern economists and replaced with a theory called "marginal utility".

Negative Ideology

Economist Milton Friedman believes that free markets are the best way to run an economy that benefits everyone. Marx and Engels did not write very much about how a real communist economy would work, making socialism a "negative ideology", meaning that it describes what should not be done but not what needs to be done to remedy the situation. They wrote about what to get rid of but not what to replace it with.

Individualists

Individualists disagree with the basic theory that people are controlled by common socio-economic forces. Instead, they believe that individuals are, and should be, free to make their own economic decisions.

Social Democrats

Social democrats and democratic socialists argue with the idea that class conflict and violent revolution are necessary to achieve socialism.

Anarchists

Anarchists believe that it is not necessary to have a communist transitional government, while anarcho-capitalists do not believe in socialism at all.

Other Theorists

Most of the left-leaning philosophers no longer believe in many of the fundamental Marxist theories such as historical materialism and the theory of value, even though they have also criticized capitalism using other arguments.

The Test of Time

Marx may have been a profound thinker, and his theories may have gotten him believers and followers around the world, but his predictions did not withstand the test of time.

Capitalist economies have changed since Marx's lifetime, and competition has not led entirely to monopolies. Wages have continued to increase, while profit rates have not decreased.

Even though the worldwide economy is in a recession and the "Occupy" movement and 99%-ers have become disgruntled, they have yet to stage a real, major, violent revolution, and most economists believe that these recessions and depressions are an unintended result of monetary policies of central bank and government "tax and spend" policies.

While there have been socialist revolutions in various locations around the world, none of them have taken place in industrialized capitalist countries as Marx predicted. In fact, most socialist countries had socialism forced upon them in poor, economically disadvantaged countries. Additionally, such socialist revolutions failed miserably to create the non-alienated, emancipated masses; rather, it enslaved and imprisoned them in gulags and political prisons.

On the other hand, even though the economy is currently depressed or in a recession, free-market countries that allowed people to own private property and retain ownership of the products and ideas that they created continue to thrive and maintain political freedom.

Conclusion

A lot of Marx's and Engels' ideas were based on their personal experiences in countries with restrictive, well-established class castes. In a society that rewards entrepreneurs such as the U.S., anyone is free to move from worker to capitalist. Many billionaires, at least the ones who didn't inherit their wealth, prove that anyone with a lot of hard work and a little bit of luck can move into the powerful ruling class. Just look at people like Bill Gates—and Richard Branson, who didn't even finish high school. There are even Chinese billionaires who studied in the US who did the same thing in a supposedly Communist society.

Marx and Engels may have sincerely believed that their ideas would benefit workers, and they may have had the best interests of the workers in mind, but their ideas have just not proven practical.

What Marx and his followers failed to take into consideration was real human behavior. Marx's theories of value and his philosophy of human nature claimed to offer a brave new world in which everyone would live together in peace, harmony, and prosperity.

As we have seen by the collapse of communism and the Soviet Union, the fall of the Berlin Wall, and the opening up of the People's Republic of China to privatization and a free market economy, these theories just do not hold up in the real world.

If you enjoyed this book, look for others in the "Plain and Simple" series at BookCaps.com

Made in the USA
Middletown, DE
26 November 2016